American Girl®

Discover
Science

Contents

How to be a scientist

Scientists try to **understand the world** and how everything in it works. They work by following a step-by-step process, called the **Scientific Method**, to test their theories and ideas. When you're a scientist, these **six steps** will lead you to science success...

3
Form a theory
Now it's time do some research, and use that information to form an opinion. You might think, "My theory is that the plant will grow best on my bedroom window sill." This is called a **hypothesis**.

1
Choose a topic
Go for something that interests you—you'll be much more likely to stay interested if you're enthusiastic about the subject. For instance, if you like being in the garden, choose a project about growing plants, or local wildlife.

2
What's the problem?
Now you need a problem to solve. Think of your project as if it were a question. So for a gardening project, you could ask, "Where in my house is the best place to grow an apple seed?"

4 Test your theory

Now conduct some experiments to see if your theory is correct. So to test your seed theory, you would try to grow seeds in lots of different places, as well as in your preferred place.

5 Keep a record

It's important to note down everything you do and observe. This is so you can be sure your conclusions are reliable. It also means that other scientists can recreate your experiments and see if they come up with the same results.

6 Reach a conclusion

Analyze your results. If they are not what you expected, that's fine. Scientists learn from getting things wrong! Suppose the seed in the kitchen grew best, not the one in the bedroom? Look for reasons. Is the kitchen warmer? Does it get more sunlight? Your conclusion might be, "An apple seed grows best if it is in sunlight all day."

Be a safe scientist!

Follow these guidelines to stay safe while you experiment.

 Whenever you see this symbol in the book, it means you need to ask an adult to help you.

- Always get an adult's permission before you start experimenting.
- Ask an adult to help with anything that involves using a knife or other sharp objects.
- Don't use a stove or do anything near a fire unless you have an adult to help.
- Water, heat, chemicals, and other science stuff can damage your American Girl dolls, so make sure they are safely out of the way while you experiment.

Good vibrations!

Almost everyone likes to listen to music, whether it's rock, pop, classical, or country. Like most things in our daily lives, there's plenty of fun and fascinating **science to explore** behind music—so let's do it!

What is sound?

All music is made up of sounds. Sound is made when **something vibrates**, like a string on a guitar or the bar of a xylophone. These movements make the air vibrate, too, causing **invisible waves** that spread out everywhere. When the waves reach your ears, your brain **converts them** into sounds.

Everything, from making music to a science project, is more fun when it's done with friends!

Dolls Rock!

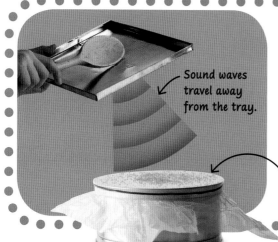

Sound waves travel away from the tray.

See sound!

For a fun way to see how **sound waves travel**, put some sugar on top of a drum. Above the sugar, bang a metal tray with a spoon and watch it jump up and down.

When the waves hit the drum's surface, it vibrates and the sugar moves.

Performing is part of music's magic—even if it's just a show for your best buddies!

Higher or lower?

The high or low sound of a musical instrument is called its pitch. You can **change the pitch** of musical instruments in different ways.

RECORDER
The column of air inside is made longer or shorter by covering the holes.

XYLOPHONE
The shorter the bar, the higher the pitch.

GUITAR
Musicians press on the strings to change their length. This alters the pitch.

DRUM
Change the pitch by making the skin tighter or looser.

8

Try it yourself!

Make it louder!

If you hum or sing down a tube, your voice sounds louder. Why do you think this is? Think about how sound waves travel in the air. Make paper tubes and cones of different lengths and shapes. Which one makes your voice loudest?

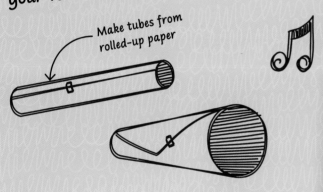

Make tubes from rolled-up paper

Water music

If you blow across the top of a bottle, you'll make a musical note. Fill bottles with different amounts of water and blow over them. Why do you think they all make different sounds?

Doll-sized science

Make **mini-headphones** so your doll can be a sound engineer in her music studio! Use a doll headband and two plastic bottle tops, covered with self-adhesive felt and glued together. For a control board, press chunky, colored pushpins into a canvas.

Sing high, sing low

Who do you think can sing the highest and lowest notes—girls, boys, men, or women? Test your friends and family to find out. Use a musical instrument to match the notes they sing. Were you correct?

Sports science

Whether playing basketball or walking the dog in the park, girls know that **exercise is fun** and makes them feel good. The body is an **amazing machine**, built to respond whenever you run, dance, jump, or swing a bat. Your heart never gets tired—in fact, the harder a heart works, the stronger it gets!

Fitness facts

During exercise, the muscles work to move the body. Muscles are **fueled by oxygen**, so the harder someone exercises, the more oxygen they need. The person breathes more quickly and deeply, and their **heart pumps faster** to supply the body's cells with oxygen from the air.

Science know-how can help you succeed at sports—but you still have to try your best and work as a team!

Feel the beat

You can feel your heart beating as it pumps blood through your body. This **regular beat is your pulse**. The easiest places to feel a pulse are on the inside of the wrists, and on either side of the neck. This is because in those places large **blood vessels**, called arteries, are just under the skin.

Place two fingers on the wrist and press lightly.

Monitor your pulse

Your resting pulse rate is the speed at which your heart beats normally, when it is not working hard. Find out your resting pulse by taking your pulse at different times (not after exercise!) and record your results.

Record your results like this

Activity	Number of beats in 10 seconds	Multiply by 6 to get resting pulse (beats per minute)
Waking up	13	78
After lunch		
Watching TV		
Playing computer games		
Just before bed		

Exercise is good for you, whether it's playing sports or walking your favorite dog!

Try it yourself!

idea
What's normal?
Do age and gender affect someone's resting pulse? Take the pulse of different people and compare your results. Use a range of volunteers to test your findings thoroughly.

Strange but true
Listening to music makes you fitter! Scientists found that people could work up to 15% harder if they listened to their favorite music while working out in the gym.

idea
Get sweaty!
Try different kinds of exercise and take your pulse afterward to see which type raises your pulse the most. You could try jumping rope, hula hooping, or running up stairs.

idea
Memory workout
Does exercise make your brain work better? Get different friends to do a memory test before exercise, and a different test afterwards. Record your results and see if there's a pattern.

idea
Practice makes perfect
Every day for two weeks, do five minutes of the same exercise. Take your pulse when you finish, then again every 30 seconds until you are back to your normal resting rate. Record your results. After two weeks, does your pulse take less time to return to normal? Does the exercise feel easier?

Look at objects on a tray for a minute. Then look away and see how many you can remember. Try it again after exercising!

Fashion sense

Fashion is fun and fabulous, but clothes play a **practical role** in your life, too. Choose clothes in fabrics to suit your activity, from tough denim for outdoor adventures to silky satin for sashaying on the dance floor. The **different qualities** of fabrics are called **properties**.

Science can help fashion fans to glitter under lights or keep cozy in the cold!

Talking textiles

Most clothes are made from **textiles**, which are the woven fibers of different materials.

ANIMAL TEXTILES
These fibers come from the wool or fur of animals like sheep, goats, or camels. Animal textiles tend to be soft and warm.

GOAT

WOOLLY SOCKS

PLANT TEXTILES
Fibers from plants such as cotton or flax are strong, and comfortable to wear.

COTTON PLANT

T-SHIRT

SYNTHETIC TEXTILES
Fabrics like nylon are made from the by-products of oil. They dry quickly and can be made waterproof.

OIL

RAINCOAT

Try it yourself!

idea
Stretch it!
Hang up a small bucket with a 6-inch length of wool. Pour in some water or sand and measure the wool's length again. Is there any change? Now try it with different yarns.

idea
Keeping warm
Wrap different fabrics round mugs of boiled water. Wait 30 minutes, then measure the temperature in each mug. Which fabric has kept the water warmest?

idea
Waterproof test
Cover empty jam jars with different fabrics, then place them in a sink and pour water onto the fabric. How much water ends up in each jar?

Secure the fabric with a rubber band.

Creative colors

Whether it's delicate, pastel portraits or bright, bold collages, painting is a fun way to **explore your creativity**. Art is also a great starting point to discover the science behind the colors in the world—from finding out what makes a rainbow, to exploring ways of making paints.

What is color?

Color comes from light, which is a form of energy. Like sound, light **travels in waves**. The different colors you can see are made by light waves of different sizes (wavelengths). An object looks a certain color because its surface **absorbs some wavelengths** and bounces others back to your eyes.

Budding artists bring their ideas
to life with beautiful paint colors
created by scientific research.

Mix it up!

Did you know you can make any color in the world from just three colors: red, blue, and yellow? Mixing them together in different proportions produces millions of shades.

Mixing paints on a palette means you can get the exact shade you need.

PRIMARY AND SECONDARY COLORS

Red, blue, and yellow are the **primary colors**. They cannot be mixed from any other colors. Orange, purple, and green are **secondary colors**. They are made by mixing two primary colors.

Red + yellow = orange
Red + blue = purple
Blue + yellow = green

Mix all three primary colors to make black.

Separating colors

This shows how a colored marker pen is actually a mixture of different colored inks. Wet blotting paper soaks up some colors faster than others, so the ink separates into different colors. This technique for separating mixtures is called chromatography.

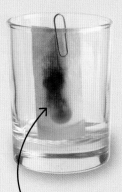

Draw a dot on blotting paper, then dip it in shallow water.

Artists and scientists are not so different! They're both good at observing carefully and recording what they see.

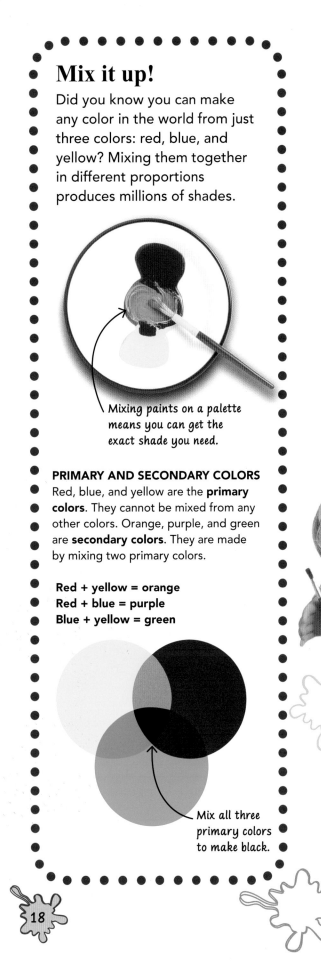

Try it yourself!

idea
Seeing colors

Show this image to different people. Can everyone see the number "7"? If not, does gender or age group make a difference to what they see? Research color-blindness to find out why!

idea
Natural pigments

Make your own paints by mashing up foods such as raspberries and beetroot, mixing coffee granules with water, or crushing flower petals in oil. Paint your colors on paper and leave them in sunlight for a few days. Which color stays brightest and which fades most?

Some people can't see a difference between red and green. →

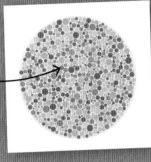

idea
Soap rainbow

Pour some milk onto a plate. Add a few drops of blue, red, and yellow food coloring to the milk, near the middle. Now squeeze a drop of dish soap into the center. What happens? Do some research and see if you can find out why!

Doll-sized science

Make your doll a **museum conservator**, using science to restore old paintings. Make her some cool magnifying eyewear by gluing a pocket magnifyer to some alligator clips, then clipping them onto some doll eyeglasses.

Science on the menu

Cooking is an important skill, and it's fun to get creative in the kitchen or barbecue in the backyard. Science helps you to understand **how food works** so that you can choose the best foods to **help your body** to function well, grow, and repair itself.

Why eat food?

Food is made of many different substances, called nutrients. To **release the nutrients** so that they can be used by the body, food has to be broken down into its smallest form. The body processes food by chopping, crushing, and churning it, and also by using chemicals called enzymes. This **essential process** is called digestion.

Cooking healthy, tasty meals is another way to combine your creative and scientific talents!

Types of food

People need to eat a **range of types of food** in order to get all the nutrients they need. Some nutrients provide energy, some help to make bones and organs strong, and others work to repair damage and fight illnesses.

Carbohydrates from cereals, rice, and potatoes give energy.

Protein from meat, eggs, and beans help to build and repair bodies.

Fats from milk, butter, and oil help vitamins reach the body's cells.

Fruit and vegetables provide vital vitamins and minerals.

Food for energy

Everyone knows you need energy to move, but sleeping, breathing, or thinking uses up energy, too! Scientists use **calories** to measure the amount of **energy in food**. The foods below have something in common— they all contain 100 calories!

BOILED EGG

4 SQUARES OF CHOCOLATE

BANANA

GLASS OF ORANGE JUICE

Using up energy can be fun, especially when you're roller-skating!

Try it yourself!

idea · Tongue test

Are some parts of the tongue better at detecting certain tastes than others? Add sugar, salt, lemon juice, and soy sauce to different glasses of water. Ask friends to use cotton swabs to dab the solutions on different parts of their tongue. What's the result?

idea · Tasty colors

Does the color of a food affect how people think it tastes? Put different food colorings in plain yogurt, then ask friends to identify which tastes they can detect. Does the yellow yogurt taste of lemon, or the red of strawberry? Or does it make no difference?

idea · Low fat, high fat

Can people tell the difference between regular and low-fat foods? You could test things like potato chips, cheese, milk, or cookies. Does the tasters' age or gender make any difference to results?

TOP TIP
Before you begin, make sure your tasting volunteers don't have any food allergies!

Strange but true

An ordinary potato is crammed with nutrients. As well as vitamins B, C, and D, it also contains iron, calcium, magnesium, and potassium. Yum!

---

idea · Best breakfast

Food labels help people make choices about which foods to eat. Compare different breakfast items to find out which contain the most—or least—sugar.

Check the sugar content of different cereals, breads, and fruits.

Science camp

There's no better way to get **close to nature** than camping. The simple life is a challenge—but if you **apply a little science**, you can make sure you stay warm, dry, and well-fed!

Science helps explorers bring a few home comforts to the great outdoors!

Keep cool naturally

There's no refrigerator on a campground, but with a bit of science know-how you can keep favorite drinks cool even on the hottest day. As water evaporates, it **draws heat away** from its surroundings. This principle can be used to set up a DIY refrigerator.

1. Put a can of soda in a glass dish, then cover the can with a terracotta flowerpot. Now spray cold water all over the pot, until it's fully soaked.

2. Keep the pot wet by spraying it with water every so often. As the water evaporates from the surface of the pot, it draws heat from inside it, keeping your can cool!

Try it yourself!

idea Fresh food

What's the best way to keep foods fresh? Try storing a strawberry in paper or plastic bags, aluminum foil, and plastic wrap. Check on the strawberries every day and record your results.

idea Marshmallow trial

✋ Which part of a fire is hottest? Put marshmallows on sticks and ask an adult to hold them to different parts of the campfire. You'll soon find the best way to cook s'mores!

idea Bug watch

Conduct a night-bug survey. Turn on a flashlight and place it upright in the ground. Then observe and record the different bugs that are attracted by the light.

Feel the force!

When ballet dancers jump, twirl, or balance, there are forces at work, helping them to leap higher or hold a pose. Forces are the **hidden power** behind everything around us—from you pushing open a door, to the **pull of gravity** that keeps Earth going around the Sun.

What is a force?

A force is simply a **push or a pull**. Forces make things move and they also cause things to go slower or faster, or come to a stop. A force can make an object **change direction** or even **change its shape**. Most forces work when they touch an object, such as when you kick a ball. Other forces, such as gravity or magnetism, can work at a distance.

Powerful forces, such as gravity, are at work when dancers make their leaps and movements.

What is gravity?

Gravity is the pulling force that makes objects fall when you drop them. Earth's gravity pulls everything toward its center—without it, we would float into space! When you weigh things, you are measuring the amount of pulling force (gravity) on that object.

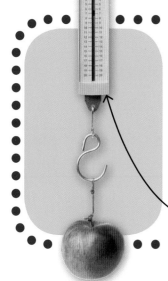

The scale measures how much the apple is pulled down by gravity.

Remember the rules!

There are three simple ideas that can help you to understand how forces affect the way things move.

RULE 1

If something is not moving, it will **stay still** until a force acts on it. If it is moving, it will carry on until another force makes it change its motion.

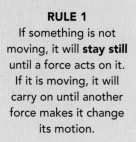

The dancer stays still because nothing is pushing or pulling him.

RULE 2

When a force is applied to an object, it **moves in the same direction** as the force. A force can make a moving object go faster, slow down, or change direction.

The dancer's muscles apply upward force to raise her leg.

RULE 3

Forces always **happen in pairs**. This means that whenever a force acts in one direction, it creates another force in the opposite direction.

When a dancer pushes down hard on the floor, the floor pushes back, making her jump in the air.

When a snowboard rubs against the snow, it creates a force called friction. This slows it down. Smooth snow creates only a little friction, so you can glide easily!

Try it yourself!

idea
Pushing power

Try pushing down on bathroom scales. The display will show you how hard you are pushing. Can you push harder with your whole hand or with one finger? Who can push the strongest in your family?

idea
Ramp it up

Investigate how gravity works on slopes. Make different ramps with some books and a board. Roll the same toy car down each one and time the journeys. Do steeper slopes make the car go faster or slower?

Place the car on the slope and let go. Don't push!

idea
Causing friction

Now cover your sloping board with different things like cotton, sandpaper, or plastic. Do the surfaces slow down or speed up the car?

Doll-sized science

Make a cute mini car to use in your experiments. Use two round lollipop sticks for the axles and push each stick through a two-inch section of a straw. Put a wooden craft wheel on the ends the sticks, then glue a bead onto each end. Glue the axles to a clothespin—and you're ready for a test drive!

What's the matter?

If you have ever frozen fruit juice to make a popsicle, you've made a **liquid change into a solid**. Many of the things around us can change, depending on things like temperature or being put under pressure. Let's find out how these transformations happen!

What is matter?

Everything in the world is made of matter. Matter mostly exists in three states: **solid**, **liquid**, or **gas**. Matter can pass from one state to another if the conditions around it change. For example, **water is a liquid** at room temperature. It changes into solid ice at low temperatures, and at high temperatures it evaporates and becomes a gas—steam.

A day in the sun is much more fun when there are ice-cold popsicles to enjoy!

Solid, liquid, gas

When a solid is heated, the particles that make it up begin to vibrate. Then the particles start to flow around each other and the solid becomes liquid. Eventually, the particles break free of each other and the liquid becomes a gas.

Particles hold tightly together in a grid shape.

SOLID
A solid, such as ice, holds its shape on its own.

Particles are held together more loosely.

LIQUID
A liquid, such as water, takes the shape of its container.

Particles are moving too quickly to hold together.

GAS
A gas, such as steam, spreads out to fill the available space.

All change!

Water can change from solid to liquid to gas and back again. We call this a **reversible change**. Some changes are irreversible. When you heat wood so it burns, it turns to ash. When the ash cools down, it can't turn back into wood.

Burning wood changes it into ash and smoke.

On a warm day, ice cream won't stay solid for long. Better get to work!

Try it yourself!

idea Freeze right there!
Do some liquids take longer to freeze than others? Find out by filling ice-cube trays with different liquids, such as orange juice, heavy cream, salt water, and low-fat milk. Check on them every hour to see how long each liquid takes to freeze.

Strange but true
Ice melts into liquid water at 0°C, but a metal called tungsten melts at a scorching 3,422°C!

idea Milk to butter
Chilling isn't the only thing that changes liquids into solids. Put some heavy cream in a jar and screw the lid on tight. Now shake... and shake... and shake! Every five minutes, stop and check the contents. Eventually, you'll have butter!

idea What changes?
Get an adult to help you heat some foods, to find which change irreversibly and which change back when they are cool again. You could try heating chocolate or cheese in a microwave oven, poaching an egg, or putting bread in a toaster.

idea Grow a crystal
Turn sugary water into solid crystals! Get an adult to help you heat water, food coloring, and sugar to make a syrup. Place a popsicle stick into the mixture. After a few days, crystals should form around the stick.

Pet power

Girls love to pamper their pooches—but pets also make a super study subject for budding scientists! The **science of living things** is called **biology**. Biologists specialize in different areas, and someone who studies animals is a zoologist.

Strong, sturdy bulldogs were originally used for guarding property.

Everyone likes to look and feel their best—that's why pups love the grooming parlor!

Labradors are calm. They make great service dogs, helping people with things they can't do alone.

Border Collies are intelligent and lively. They often help farmers to herd farm animals.

Huskies are strong sled dogs. Their super-thick fur keeps them warm in Arctic winters.

Super sense

Humans get most of their information about their surroundings from seeing. But dogs are different—they use their noses to collect data! A human's nose has six million smell-detectors, but a dog's has more than 300 million!

A dog uses its nose to track down food, find its way, and locate other dogs—or you!

Try it yourself!

idea

Sniff it out

What scents are dogs most interested in? Put different things in bowls and see which ones the dog visits first. You could try fruit, meat, an item of your clothing, a plastic toy, or another dog's collar.

idea

New tricks

Test out some friendly dogs to find out which can learn a new trick the fastest. Does one breed do better than the others? Does a dog's age or size make any difference?

Doll-sized science

Build a **scaled-down veterinary surgery** so your doll can care for her favorite pets. Make tiny animal bandages from washi tape. Pony bead lacing makes a good stethoscope, with glued-on mini flowerpots as earpieces and a bead for the chestpiece.

Kitchen lab

Baking is fun to do—and it's even more fun to eat and share the results! But did you know that when you bake, you are actually **doing chemistry**? Let's look at the science behind those fluffy muffins and crunchy cookies...

What is a chemical reaction?

When substances change to form a new substance, we call it a **chemical reaction**. All substances are made of groups of atoms that bond together. In baking, the heat breaks the bonds between the ingredients' atoms. The atoms then mix and **form new bonds**. So flour, yeast, and water are transformed... into delicious bread!

Anyone who thinks chemistry isn't fun has never baked cupcakes with a special friend!

Rising reaction

The special ingredient that makes bread rise is a living organism called yeast. When it's mixed with flour and water, yeast releases bubbles of a gas called carbon dioxide. These bubbles make the bread dough expand and rise to twice its size.

Warm water and yeast

Risen dough

Flour added to mixture to make dough

Cake chemistry

A cake is the delicious result of many different chemical reactions between a variety of ingredients.

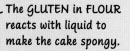

The GLUTEN in FLOUR reacts with liquid to make the cake spongy.

BUTTER OR FAT stops the gluten from reacting too much, which would make the cake tough.

BAKING SODA reacts to form bubbles, which make the cake rise.

SUGAR adds sweetness, and binds with other ingredients to make the surface brown.

EGGS react to heat by becoming solid, giving the cake texture.

Always follow a recipe carefully to avoid chemical catastrophes!

Try it yourself!

idea Rise up!
Combine yeast with warm water and flour in three different bowls. Put each one in a different place, such as a refrigerator, a sunny window, and a cupboard. After 30 minutes, check on them. In which place did the dough rise most? Why do you think that is?

idea Leave it out
✋ How vital are cake ingredients? Make a batch of cupcakes, using your favorite recipe. Now make three small batches, each leaving out one ingredient, such as eggs, baking powder, or butter. How different do the cakes taste and look?

TOP TIP
Remember to wash your hands before you get busy in the kitchen!

---

idea Gluten-free test
✋ Test how using gluten-free flour affects the height of cupcakes. Do they rise more or less than a cupcake made with regular flour? Is the taste the same?

idea Soda fountain!
✋ Here's a way to test the power of baking soda. Pour some warm water into a plastic bottle. Add some baking soda and a squirt of dishwashing liquid. Now pour in some vinegar and quickly put a cork in the bottle. What happens? Do you get the same result if you leave any ingredients out?

Stand well back after you've put the cork in!

Rain or shine

The weather affects us all. For instance, rain helps a farmer grow crops, but too much can cause chaos and floods. Many people rely on scientists **predicting the weather** to help them do their jobs or keep safe. The study of weather is called meteorology.

Rain alert!
You should never get your doll wet. Make sure she's safely out of the way when you're splashing in puddles.

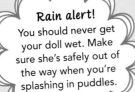

A rainy day is a perfect chance for young meteorologists—and their helper—to do some practical research!

Up in the clouds

Clouds are made up of tiny droplets of water or ice crystals. When warm weather makes water evaporate from the ocean, it rises up into the atmosphere as gas (vapor). The higher it gets, the more the vapor cools down. It then turns back into droplets and makes clouds. There are three basic types of cloud: flat, grey **stratus** clouds, wispy **cirrus** clouds, and puffy **cumulus** clouds.

STRATUS
These blankets of cloud hang low in the sky.

CIRRUS
Cirrus are wispy clouds that sit very high up in the atmosphere.

CUMULUS
These cotton-ball clouds are the type of cloud that produces rain.

Try it yourself!

idea
Cloud watching
Take photos or draw the different clouds you observe, and make a note of the weather on those days. How different are the clouds on dry and rainy days?

idea
Who gets it right?
Compare two or more TV or newspaper weather forecasts over two weeks. Does one forecast do better than others?

idea
Hot and cold
What time of day is usually the hottest or coolest? Take outdoor thermometer readings every hour over a few days, then analyze your results.

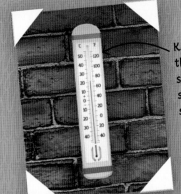

Keep your thermometer in the same place, ideally somewhere that's shady all day.

Nature spotting

Nature is all around you, whether you're out and about in the city or camping in the wilderness. If you're patient and very quiet, you'll be amazed at what you can discover about **birds, bugs, and beasts** and how they live.

What is a habitat?

A habitat is any place where an animal or plant can find the essentials it **needs to survive**, including food, water, and shelter. Habitats range from frozen seas to scorching deserts—even a city street is a habitat! Some biologists study habitats and the **adaptations** animals make to live in them.

Camping is a great way to spot wildlife, especially shy creatures that only appear after dark!

Amazing Amazon

One of the planet's most important habitats is the **tropical rainforest** around the giant Amazon river in South America. This area contains an incredible one-third of all the world's animal and plant species. The trees in the Amazon also produce one-fifth of all the oxygen that we breathe in the air. Thanks, trees!

More than 400 different species of frog live in the Amazon rainforest.

Animal tracking

Some animals are so shy that you'll never see them. If you're sharp-eyed, though, you might spot their tell-tale footprints. Here are some tracks to look out for next time you're out hiking.

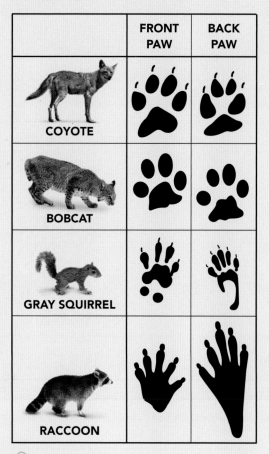

	FRONT PAW	BACK PAW
COYOTE		
BOBCAT		
GRAY SQUIRREL		
RACCOON		

Smart girls stay safe on nature rambles. Always take water to drink, a compass, and a headlamp.

Try it yourself!

💡 idea
Backyard bugwatch

Conduct your own bug survey! Study a 1-foot square patch of earth in your neighborhood and see how many different creatures you can find. Do the same a month later and compare results.

💡 idea
Night visitors

Which animals visit when you're asleep? Spread some sand in an area of your backyard, and put one dish of dog food and one of fruit in the middle of the sand. In the morning, check for footprints. Can you work who came for a midnight feast?

💡 idea
Nature survey

Set aside a half hour at the same time on different days and see how many different animals you can spot in one particular place, like the local park. Note things that might affect your results, like the weather, or how many people are around.

Doll-sized science

If you love science and the outdoors, cartography (map-making) might be for you! Make your doll a safety vest by folding five 16-inch pieces of duct tape in half lengthways. Tape three strips together to make the back. Now attach a strip on each side, along the top. Fold a 24-inch piece of tape in half and tape it round the bottom, to make armholes.

Grow your garden

Gardens aren't just for playing, reading, or relaxing in! There's so much to find out about the **amazing plants and trees** around you. Whether you want to grow beautiful blooms, scrumptious salads, or healing herbs, a little **scientific know-how** will help you on your way.

What is a plant?

A plant is a **living thing** that is usually rooted in the ground. Like other living things plants need food to survive, but unlike animals, **plants make their own food** from the Sun's rays. There are many of types of plant and they can look quite different, but they all need the same basic things to survive.

A flower-filled garden can be paradise for for birds, bees, butterflies—and you, too!

Plant parts

To survive and grow, a plant needs light, water, nutrients (food), and oxygen. There are nearly 400,000 kinds of plant, from tall trees to tiny meadow flowers. Almost all of them have the same basic parts.

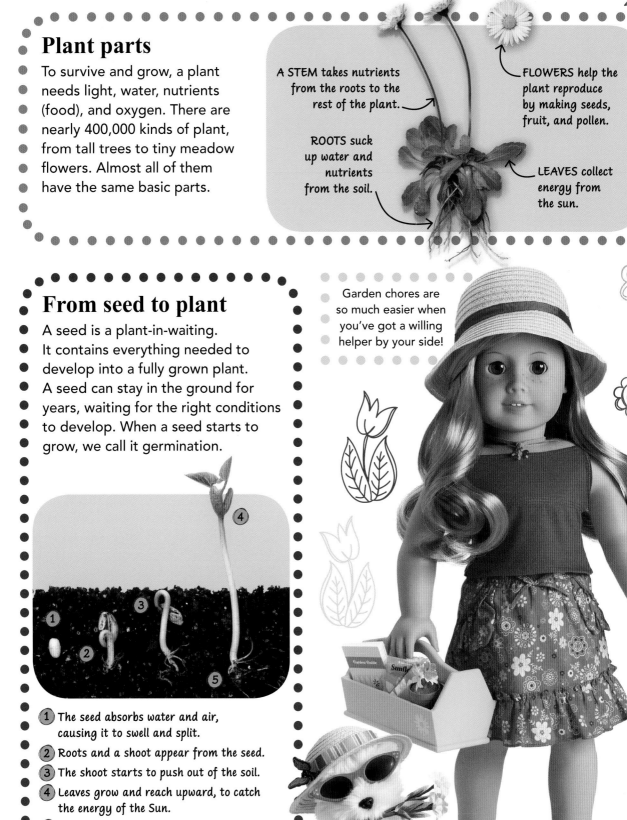

A STEM takes nutrients from the roots to the rest of the plant.

ROOTS suck up water and nutrients from the soil.

FLOWERS help the plant reproduce by making seeds, fruit, and pollen.

LEAVES collect energy from the sun.

From seed to plant

A seed is a plant-in-waiting. It contains everything needed to develop into a fully grown plant. A seed can stay in the ground for years, waiting for the right conditions to develop. When a seed starts to grow, we call it germination.

Garden chores are so much easier when you've got a willing helper by your side!

1. The seed absorbs water and air, causing it to swell and split.
2. Roots and a shoot appear from the seed.
3. The shoot starts to push out of the soil.
4. Leaves grow and reach upward, to catch the energy of the Sun.
5. Roots keep the plant firmly in the ground.

Try it yourself!

Sun-seeking plants
✋ Put a small houseplant in a shoe box, cut a hole in the side of the box and put the lid on. Water the plant regularly. Note what happens over the next few weeks. Clue: a plant will do whatever it can to find sunlight!

Watch a flower drink
Add different food colorings to glasses of water, and put a cut white flower in each. After a few days, what happens to the petals?

Strange but true
The tallest plant in the world is the Coast Redwood tree, which grows in California. It reaches 380 ft—that's taller than the Statue of Liberty!

Grow a fruit
Plant an avocado pit in a pot and put it on a sunny windowsill. Water it regularly and watch it grow! You could also try peach pits, and apple or lemon seeds.

Sprouting seeds
If you put a seed in a jar filled with paper towels soaked in water, it will germinate. Test other liquids to see if they can germinate a seed, too. You could use things like milk, fruit juice, cooking oil, or soda.

The top half of the avocado pit should show above the soil.

Science spa

Even during a pampering session, there are **questions all around** for young scientists to ponder. What are bubbles made of? Why does a rubber duck float? Let's investigate!

Water warning!
Don't put your doll in real water—she's designed for dry land only!

Fill your bathtub with bubbles, relax, and wait for inspiration to strike!

The small ball of clay displaces little water, so it sinks.

Sink or float?

An object floats or sinks depending on something called **displacement**. When you put something in water, it pushes some of the water out of the way (displaces it). If the displaced water **weighs more than the object** itself, the object will float.

The dish-shaped clay displaces more water, so it floats.

Water pushes upward

Try it yourself!

Strange but true

There is a legend that the ancient Greek scientist Archimedes was sitting in the bath when he figured out what makes things float or sink!

idea
Float an egg
What kind of liquid does an egg float best in? Try different things, such as plain, salty, or sugary water, or cooking oil.

idea
Blow bubbles!
Add things like sugar, lemon, and corn syrup to bubble solution, then get blowing. Which mix makes the bounciest, longest-lasting bubbles?

idea
Design a boat
Which shape of boat can carry the most weight? Make different-shaped boats with modeling clay and see how many marbles it takes to make each boat sink.

Experiment with a square, a diamond or even a donut shape.

TOP TIP
To make really long-lasting bubbles, make up your bubble-blowing solution with glycerine, and leave it for a day or two to mix well.

Seaside science

Everyone loves a fun day by the sea! From snorkeling to beachcombing, there's so much to **see and do**. But can a day at the beach inspire you to think about science, too? Yes, it can!

What is a beach?

A beach is an area of land next to a body of water, such as the sea. This land is covered with sand or pebbles, created by the **action of waves**, which slowly breaks down larger rocks and shells. This wearing away is called **erosion**.

The beach is a great place to kick back with friends—and study the shoreline, too!

How erosion works

On a beach, the sea's waves relentlessly pound rocks into smaller and smaller pieces. Eventually, they become grains of sand. On some beaches, you can see rocks at all the stages of this process.

ROCKS　　**PEBBLES**　　**SHINGLE**　　**SAND**

What are tidepools?

Tidepools are small pools left behind on the beach after the tide has gone out. Sea creatures can often be found in them.

STARFISH
Starfish have an eye at the end of each arm, and a mouth on their underside. Instead of swimming, they crawl slowly across the seabed.

HERMIT CRAB
The hermit crab lives inside the discarded shell of another animal. When it outgrows its shell, it finds a larger one to move into.

MUSSELS
Mussels are related to clams and oysters. They have a tough shell, and attach themselves to rocks and other hard surfaces in the sea.

A snorkel, swimsuit, and sunscreen are essentials for seaside wildlife watching.

54

Try it yourself!

Melting away
idea

Shells dissolve in acid. Try putting a seashell in a glass of vinegar and see what happens. Then try another acid, like lemon juice. Are the results different?

What's in the water?
idea

Ever wondered what is in seawater? Collect some and let it dry out in a shallow dish on a window sill. Is there anything left behind once the water evaporates?

Cold ocean
idea

Even when the temperature is below 0°C, the salt in seawater stops it from freezing. But how much salt is needed for this to happen? Find out by adding different amounts of salt to water in a ice cube tray, then putting in a freezer overnight.

Underwater wildlife
idea

Tidepools can be hard to see into because sunlight reflects off the water. A viewer, made by covering one end of a tube with plastic wrap, gives a clearer view. Record the marine life that you spot at different times of the day, or in different seasons.

TOP TIP
Tidepools can be slippery, so take care. Always check the time of high tide so you can leave well before then.

Stargazing

There's a **whole Universe** out there! Even without a telescope, on a clear night you can easily spot the moon, planets, and stars. The **patterns of the stars** have fascinated people for thousands of years. Let's take a look!

What is astronomy?

Astronomy is the **study of stars**, planets, and the Universe. Around 400 years ago, the invention of the telescope meant that astronomers could observe the skies in more detail. Studying the **movements of planets** and stars also helps scientists understand more about planet Earth and its place in the Universe.

A slumber party is the perfect time for a fun stargazing session!

57

Be an astronomer

You can spot amazing things in the night sky, even without a telescope. Some can be seen with the naked eye, and others with the help of binoculars. The darker the sky, the more you will see, so pick a night with a new moon and a place with no artificial lights, if you can.

BINOCULARS
A pair of binoculars will help you see more in the sky than you could by just using your eyes.

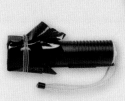

FLASHLIGHT
Cover the end with red cellophane so that you can see where you are going whilst your eyes are still adapted to the dark.

STAR MAP
You can use a paper star map (planisphere) or download an app to help you find your way around the stars.

Constellations

In ancient times, astronomers noticed that some stars appear to form patterns. They drew imaginary lines between the stars, forming images to help them remember the groups, which are called constellations. We still use these images today.

A telescope and a cozy sweater are essentials for star-spotting under the night skies!

The constellation **Canis Major** forms the shape of a dog.

Sirius is the brightest star in the sky.

Orion is visible from almost everywhere on Earth. These stars make the shape of an ancient hunter carrying a club and a shield.

Try it yourself!

idea
Changing Moon

Every night for a month, draw a picture or take a photo of the Moon, if it's visible. Does its shape change? Do research to find out why you see less or more of it at different times.

Day 1   Day 7   Day 10   Day 20   Day 24

idea
Planet paths

Some planets, like Venus and Mars, can be seen without a telescope. You could use an app to help you find them. Do they appear in the same place in the sky every night?

idea
Colorful stars

Not all stars are the same color. Use a star map and see if you can find different-colored stars, such as orange Betelgeuse, light blue Rigel, or yellow Altair.

Doll-sized science

This **mini solar system** will give you and your doll hours of awesome astronomy fun! Use a 3-inch Styrofoam ball for the Sun, and different-sized beads for the planets. Ask an adult to help you hang them with fishing wire from a painted wooden dowel. Make the rings of Saturn by gluing a hair-tie around one of the beads.

Glossary

Acid
A chemical that tastes sour, stings, or can dissolve other things. Lemon juice and vinegar are weak acids, so they are safe in foods. Strong acids can be very harmful.

Adaptation
The ways in which an animal changes and becomes better suited to the habitat it lives in.

Artery
A large blood vessel that carries blood from the heart to the rest of the body.

Atmosphere
A layer of air and other gases that surrounds planets such as Earth.

Atom
The smallest possible particle of matter. Everything in our world is made up of atoms.

Carbohydrates
A group of foods, which includes starch and sugar, that is used by the body to make energy.

Cell
One of the trillions of microscopic units that make up our bodies, and those of all living things.

Chemistry
A branch of science that studies what substances are made of and how they react with each other.

Compound
A substance made when two or more elements are joined by a chemical reaction.

Digestion
The process of breaking down food into simple nutrients so they can be absorbed into the bloodstream and carried around the body.

Enzyme
A substance that speeds up chemical reactions in the body, such as digestion.

Erosion
The wearing away of rock caused by water, wind, or weather.

Evaporation
What happens when a substance changes from a liquid to a gas, for instance when water is heated and becomes steam.

Freezing
The process that turns water into solid ice at 0°C (32°F).

Friction
A force caused by two objects rubbing or sliding together. Friction slows things down and also generates heat.

Gravity
An invisible force that pulls objects together. The Earth's gravity keeps us from falling off it!

Hypothesis
A idea, or theory, about how things work. Scientists test their hypotheses by carrying out experiments.

Magnetism
An invisible force that pulls certain metals toward each other, or pushes them apart.

Molecule
A group of atoms that have bonded together to make a new substance.

Nutrient
A substance that a plant or animal needs in order to survive and grow.

Organism
A living thing, such as a plant or animal.

Oxygen
A gas that makes up about one-fifth of the air that we breathe. Our body cells use oxygen to release energy from the food we eat.

Particle
A tiny amount of matter, such as a single atom or a group of atoms (molecule).

Pigment
A compound (mixture of chemicals) that gives something its color.

Planet
A large, round object, such as Earth, which goes around (orbits) a star, such as the Sun.

Pollen
Tiny, dust-like grains produced by flowers and spread by insects or the wind. They help flowers to produce new flowers (reproduce).

Proteins
Vital nutrients in food that help our bodies grow and repair themselves.

Rainforest
An area that receives constant, heavy rain, which allows many different trees and plants to grow into thick forest. Most rainforests are also very warm.

Reflection
The change in direction of a wave, such as a light wave, when it hits a surface.

Reproduction
The way living things make new living things, using seeds or eggs.

Scientific Method
A step-by-step process of experiments and observations. It is used by scientists to test their ideas to find out whether they are true or false

Sound wave
An invisible energy wave that is formed when a noise is made. When it reaches your ear, the wave is converted into a sound you hear.

Synthetic
Describes something that is made by humans; rather than something that occurs in the natural world.

Vitamins
A group of different substances in food that the body needs in order to work properly.

Universe
All the things that exist everywhere, including Earth and everything on it, and also all the planets, stars, and galaxies in space.

Wavelength
The distance between the highest points of two waves. In sound waves, the wavelength determines the pitch of a sound—how high or low it sounds.

Index

Acknowledgments

Penguin Random House

Senior Editor Rona Skene
Senior Designer Lisa Robb
Editor Rosie Peet
Designers Samantha Richiardi, Elena Jarmoskaite, James McKeag
Pre-Production Producer Siu Chan
Producer Louise Daly
Managing Editor Paula Regan
Managing Art Editor Jo Connor
Art Director Lisa Lanzarini
Publisher Julie Ferris
Publishing Director Simon Beecroft

Written by Rona Skene and Rosie Peet
Science consultant Ben Morgan

Printed and bound in China

www.americangirl.com
www.dk.com

A WORLD OF IDEAS:
SEE ALL THERE IS TO KNOW

DK would like to thank the following people at American Girl and
Mattel: Alex Belmonte, Alyssa Statz, Barbara Stretchberry, Riley
Wilkinson, Jodi Goldberg, Isa Primavera, Charnita Belcher,
Kristine Lombardi, and Nancy Price.

Thanks also to Hannah Gulliver-Jones for editorial assistance,
and Julia March for proofreading and indexing.

Photo credits
8 (l), **12** (tl), **13** (br) DK archive; **15** (tl) Dorling Kindersley: Peter
Anderson/Odds Farm Park, other images on this page DK archive;
18 (t, l), **19**, **22**, **23**, **25**, **28** DK archive; **32** (l) Dorling Kindersley:
Dave King/The Science Museum, (tr) DK archive; **33**, **35**, **38**, **39**
DK archive; **41** (b) DK archive; **44** (t) Dorling Kindersley: Thomas
Marent, (l) Dorling Kindersley: Andy and Gill Swash; **48**, **49**, **51**,
54, **55**, **58** DK archive.
For further information see www.dkimages.com

All other images © American Girl